Git Version Control Guide
Step –by-step tutorial for beginners

Table of Contents

Introduction

With modern projects, development usually involves several users. The problem comes in defining how the various users involved in the project can make their contribution. In most cases, the developers are not located in a central place, but they are distributed. In such cases, there is a need for us to come up with a mechanism which will help us bring all of these developers together. Git is one of the platforms which can help us to easily do this. This book guides you on how to use Git for this purpose. Enjoy reading!

Chapter 1- How to use Git for Development

The Command Line

There are a number of ways that we can use Git. There are original command line tools, as well as several graphical user interfaces (GUI), providing us with different capabilities. The command line provides you with an environment in which you can run all of your Git commands. In most cases, the GUI will only have a subset of the functionalities of Git, meaning that yoou cannot do much with it. With knowledge on how to operate the command line, you will find it easy for you to use the GUI, but the reverse is not necessarily true. Although you may choose to use the GUI version, remember that the command line is readily installed and available for your use.

Installing Git

Before you can begin to use Git, you should first make it available on your computer. Also, if you have already installed this, it will be good for you to update it to the latest version. It can be installed as a package, by using another installer, or by downloading the source code and then compiling it by yourself.

Installation in Linux

For you to use an installer to install Git tools in Linux, you can make use of the basic package management-tool which comes with the distribution. For Fedora users, you can use the "yum" command as shown below:

$ sudo yum install git-all

For a Debian distribution such as Ubuntu, use the command given below:

$ sudo apt-get install git-all

Installation on Mac

Installation of Git on a Mac can be done in a number of ways. The easiest way is by use of the Xcode command line tools. If you want to install a version which is more updated, use the binary installer.

Installing from Source

Some people may choose to install the Git from the source, since you will install the latest version of Git. For you to install the Git from the source, you must have installed the libraries which Git depends on, and these include curl, openssl, expat, zlib, and libiconv. If you are using a distribution with apt-get or yum, then you can choose to use any of the following commands to install the necessary dependencies:

**$ sudo yum install curl-devel expat-devel gettext-devel **

** openssl-devel perl-devel zlib-devel**
**$ sudo apt-get install libcurl4-gnutls-dev libexpat1-dev gettext **

** libz-dev libssl-dev**

For you to be in a position to add the documentation in various formats such as info, htmo, or doc, the following additional dependencies will have to be added:

$ sudo yum install asciidoc xmlto docbook2X
$ sudo apt-get install asciidoc xmlto docbook2x

For those using derivatives of Fedora/RHEL/RHEL-de, you have to do the following:

$ sudo ln -s /usr/bin/db2x_docbook2texi /usr/bin/docbook2x-texi

The above code is as a result of differences in binary names.

Once all of the dependencies have been set up, you can get the latest release tarball from a number of places. You can then compile and install as shown below:

```
$ tar -zxf git-2.0.0.tar.gz
$ cd git-2.0.0
$ make configure
$ ./configure --prefix=/usr
$ make all doc info
$ sudo make install install-doc install-html install-info
```

Once you are done, just use the Git to get the latest version of Git via the updates as shown below:

```
$ git clone git://git.kernel.org/pub/scm/git/git.git
```

Setting Your Identity

Once you have installed Git, you should go ahead to set your username and password. This is of importance, as each commit in Git will make use of the information.

$ git config --global user.name "John Joel"
$ git config --global user.email johnjoel@domain.com

This should only be done once, and be aware that Git will have to use that information in each of its operations.

The Editor

Once your identity has been set up, you can configure the default text editor which you will use to type in your messages. If you don't configure this, then Git will make use of your default text editor.
For you to use another text editor other than emacs, use the command given below:

$ git config --global core.editor emacs

For Windows users, who need to use a different text editor such as the Notepad++, use the following commands:

In an x86 system:

$ git config --global core.editor "'C:/Program Files/Notepad++/notepad++.exe' -multiInst -nosession"

In an x64 system:

$ git config --global core.editor "'C:/Program Files (x86)/Notepad++/notepad++.exe' -multiInst -nosession"

Checking the Settings

The command "git config –list" can be used for the purpose of checking the Git settings on your system:

```
$ git config --list
user.name=John Joel
user.email=johnjoel@domain.com
color.status=auto
color.branch=auto
color.interactive=auto
color.diff=auto
...
```

Sometimes, you may need to get help on how to use certain Git commands. There are three ways that you can get help:

```
$ git help <verb>
$ git <verb> --help
$ man git-<verb>
```

Consider the example given below on how you can get the manual pages for the "*config*" command:

```
$ git help config
```

Getting Git Repository

There are two approaches on how one can get a Git project. The first approach does this by taking an existing project or directory and then importing it into Git. The second approach involves cloning a Git repository from another server.
If you need to begin tracking a new project in Git, you should go to the directory of the project and then type the following command:

```
$ git init
```

For you to launch version-controlling existing files, you should begin by tracking the files and then perform an initial commit. This can be done by use of a few "git add" commands which should specify the files which you need to track, and then followed by a "git commit." This is shown below:

$ git add *.c
$ git add LICENSE
$ git commit -m 'initial project version'

At this point, you should have a Git repository having tracked files and an initial commit.

Cloning Existing Repository

To clone a repository, you use the command "git clone [url]."
An example of this is shown below:

$ git clone https://github.com/libgit2/libgit2
In the above command, a directory with the name "libgit2' will
be created, and then a .git directory will be initialized inside
this. If you need to clone a repository into a directory with the
name "libgit2," that can be specified as the next command line
option as shown below:

$ git clone https://github.com/libgit2/libgit2 mylibgit

Recording Changes to Repositories

Suppose that you have a Git repository and some files in it.
You need to make some changes and then commit snapshots
of the changes in the repository whenever the project reaches a
state that needs to be recorded.

The command *"git status"* can be used for the purpose of
checking the status of the files. After cloning and execution of
this command, you should get something which looks as
follows:

$ git status
On branch master
Your branch is up-to-date with 'origin/master'.
nothing to commit, working directory clean

The above message just indicates that your directory is clean
and is working as expected. Note that Git will not see any
untracked files.

Suppose you have added a new file to your project, such as a
simple file "README." If the file didn't exist before and then
you execute the command "git status," you will see the
untracked status of the command as shown below:

```
$ echo 'My Project' > README
$ git status
On branch master
Your branch is up-to-date with 'origin/master'.
Untracked files:

 (use "git add <file>..." to include in what will be
committed)

  README

nothing added to commit but untracked files present
(use "git add" to track)
```

From the result, it is very clear that the README file which you have just added remains untracked. Untracked just means that Git has seen a file which was not available in the previous snapshot, and it is good for you to remember that it will not be added to the commit snapshots until you tell it to do that.

Tracking new files

For you to begin to track a new file, you have to make use of the command *"git add."* If you need to begin tracking our previous README file, execute the following command:

$ git add README

You can then run the command for checking the status of the file, and you will find that the file falls under the tracking category and has been committed. This is shown below:

$ git status
On branch master
Your branch is up-to-date with 'origin/master'.
Changes to be committed:
  (use "git reset HEAD <file>..." to unstage)

  new file: README

Staging Modified Files

We need to change a file which is already under tracking. Once you change the file which is already under tracking and then you run the command for status, you will get some output which appears as follows:

$ git status
On branch master
Your branch is up-to-date with 'origin/master'.
Changes to be committed:
  (use "git reset HEAD <file>..." to unstage)

  new file: README

Changes not staged for commit:
  (use "git add <file>..." to update what will be committed)

  (use "git checkout -- <file>..." to discard changes in working directory)

  modified: CONTRIBUTING.md

The status of our file just means that it has been modified in our working directory, but it has not been staged. For this to be staged, do it by use of the "git add" command.

We can now run the "Git add" command followed by the "git status" command on the file:

$ git add CONTRIBUTING.md
$ git status
On branch master
Your branch is up-to-date with 'origin/master'.
Changes to be committed:
  (use "git reset HEAD <file>..." to unstage)

new file: README
modified: CONTRIBUTING.md

The files will be staged, and they will go into the next commit. You may also remember that you have a simple change to make to the file before you can commit it. You can do that by opening the file, making the change, and then committing the changes. You should then run the "git status" command one more time as shown below:

$ vim CONTRIBUTING.md
$ git status
On branch master
Your branch is up-to-date with 'origin/master'.
Changes to be committed:
** (use "git reset HEAD <file>..." to unstage)**

** new file: README**
** modified: CONTRIBUTING.md**

Changes not staged for commit:
** (use "git add <file>..." to update what will be committed)**
** (use "git checkout -- <file>..." to discard changes in working directory)**

** modified: CONTRIBUTING.md**

At this point, the file has been listed in both *"staged" and* "unstaged" status. After modifying a file after the "git add" command, you will have to run the command "git add" once again so as to stage the latest version of the file. This is shown below:

$ git add CONTRIBUTING.md
$ git status
On branch master
Your branch is up-to-date with 'origin/master'.
Changes to be committed:

(use "git reset HEAD <file>..." to unstage)

new file: README
modified: CONTRIBUTING.md
Short Status

The "git status" command gives us too much data, as it is too wordy. Git provides you with a flag for short status so that the output you get can be summarized. In such a case, we run the command "git status –s" or "git status –short." With the commands, you get a very compact output as shown below:

$ git status -s
 M README
MM Rakefile
A lib/git.rb
M lib/simplegit.rb
?? LICENSE.txt

New files which are not under tracking usually have "??" after them. This is simple on how to identify such files. New files which have just been added to the staging area usually have an "A" next to them.

Ignoring Files

Obviously, there must be some files which you don't need Git to add automatically or just show you that the files are untracked. In most cases, these are the files which are generated by the system itself, or the ones which are built in, and examples of these are the log files. This problem can be solved as shown in the problem given below:

$ cat .gitignore
*.[oa]
*~

The first line just tells Git that it should ignore any files which end with a ".o" or a ".a." Files which might result after compiling your code will also be compiled. Consider the next example given below, which demonstrates how this can be done:

 # no .a files
*.a

 # but track the lib.a, even if you are ignoring the .a files above

!lib.a

 # ignore the TODO file only in the current directory, but not subdir/TODO

/TODO

 # ignore all the files in the build/ directory
build/

 # ignore the doc/notes.txt, but not the doc/server/arch.txt

doc/*.txt

 # ignore all the .pdf files in doc/ directory
doc/**/*.pdf

Viewing the Staged and Unstaged Changes

You always need to use the "git status" command so as to check for the status of your files as well as the "git diff" command so as to know the differences between files in Git.

Suppose you have edited and staged the file README, and you have edited the file CONTRIBUTING.md without staging it. Once you execute the "Git status" command, you will get an output which appears as follows:

$ git status
On branch master
Your branch is up-to-date with 'origin/master'.
Changes to be committed:
  (use "git reset HEAD <file>..." to unstage)

   modified: README

Changes not staged for commit:
  (use "git add <file>..." to update what will be committed)

   (use "git checkout -- <file>..." to discard changes in working directory)

   modified: CONTRIBUTING.md

If you need to see the file which you have edited without staging, execute the "git diff" command as shown below:

$ git diff
diff --git a/CONTRIBUTING.md b/CONTRIBUTING.md
index 8ebb991..643e24f 100644
--- a/CONTRIBUTING.md
+++ b/CONTRIBUTING.md
@@ -65,7 +65,8 @@ branch directly, things can get messy.

Please include a nice description of your changes when you submit your PR;

if we have to read the whole diff to figure out why you're contributing

in the first place, you're less likely to get feedback and have your change

-merged in.
+merged in. Also, split your changes into comprehensive chunks if your patch is

+longer than a dozen lines.

If you are starting to work on a particular area, feel free to submit a PR

that highlights your work in progress (and note in the PR title that it's

The command works by making a comparison between what is contained in your working directory and what is contained in your staging area. The result then gives you the changes which you have done without staging.

If you need to check whatever you have changed and it should go into the next commit, use the command "git diff –staged." The command will make a comparison between the staged changes to the last commit. This is shown below:

```
$ git diff --staged
diff --git a/README b/README
new file mode 100644
index 0000000.03902a1
--- /dev/null
+++ b/README
@@ -0,0 +1 @@
+My Project
```

It is important for you to note that the "Git diff" command will not show you all the changes that you have made since the last commit, but it shows you only the changes which are unstaged.

An example is when you have staged the file "CONTRIBUDING.md" and edited it. The command "git diff" can be used for seeing the changes which are staged and the changes which are unstaged. Consider a situation in which you have the following environment:

$ git add CONTRIBUTING.md
$ echo '# test line' >> CONTRIBUTING.md
$ git status
On branch master
Your branch is up-to-date with 'origin/master'.
Changes to be committed:
  (use "git reset HEAD <file>..." to unstage)

   modified: CONTRIBUTING.md

Changes not staged for commit:
  (use "git add <file>..." to update what will be committed)
  (use "git checkout -- <file>..." to discard changes in working directory)

   modified: CONTRIBUTING.md

At this point, the command "git diff" can be used for viewing the unstaged changes. This is shown below:

$ git diff
diff --git a/CONTRIBUTING.md b/CONTRIBUTING.md
index 643e24f..87f08c8 100644
--- a/CONTRIBUTING.md
+++ b/CONTRIBUTING.md
@@ -119,3 +119,4 @@ at the

Starter Projects

See our [projects list](https://github.com/libgit2/libgit2/blob/development/PROJECTS.md).

+# test line

You can then use the command "git diff –cached" so as to see what so far has been staged. This is shown below:

```
$ git diff --cached
diff --git a/CONTRIBUTING.md
b/CONTRIBUTING.md
index 8ebb991..643e24f 100644
--- a/CONTRIBUTING.md
+++ b/CONTRIBUTING.md
@@ -65,7 +65,8 @@ branch directly, things can get
messy.
 Please include a nice description of your changes
when you submit your PR;

 if we have to read the whole diff to figure out why
you're contributing

 in the first place, you're less likely to get feedback
and have your change

-merged in.
+merged in. Also, split your changes into
comprehensive chunks if your patch is

+longer than a dozen lines.

 If you are starting to work on a particular area, feel
free to submit a PR

 that highlights your work in progress (and note in
the PR title that it's
```

Committing Changes

Now that you have set the staging area the way you need, the changes can be committed. For you to commit your changes, you just have to type "git commit."

$ git commit

Once you do that, the editor of your choice will be launched. The editor will have the following information:

 # Please enter the commit message for your changes. Lines starting

 # with '#' will be ignored, and an empty message aborts the commit.
 # On branch master
 # Your branch is up-to-date with 'origin/master'.
#
 # Changes to be committed:
 #   new file: README
 #   modified: CONTRIBUTING.md
#
~
~
~
".git/COMMIT_EDITMSG" 9L, 283C

One can also choose to type the commit message inline using the commit command by specifying it after the flag "-m" as shown below:

$ git commit -m "Story 182: Fix benchmarks for speed"

[master 463dc4f] Story 182: Fix benchmarks for speed

2 files changed, 2 insertions(+)

create mode 100644 README

At this point, you will have created your first commit. As you have seen, it has given you some output regarding itself.

Skipping Staging Area

When you add the –a flag to the Git "git commit" command, every file which is under tracking will be staged before the commit can be done, meaning that you will be allowed to skip the part for "git add." This is shown below:

$ git status
On branch master
Your branch is up-to-date with 'origin/master'.
Changes not staged for commit:
  (use "git add <file>..." to update what will be committed)

  (use "git checkout -- <file>..." to discard changes in working directory)

    modified: CONTRIBUTING.md
no changes added to commit (use "git add" and/or "git commit -a")

$ git commit -a -m 'added new benchmarks'
[master 83e38c7] added new benchmarks
1 file changed, 5 insertions(+), 0 deletions(-)

Removing Files

If you need to remove your file from Git, you should first remove it from the list of tracked files and then commit. This is done using the command "git rm," and the file is also removed from the list of untracked files, and you no longer see it in the list.

If the file is removed only from the working directory, it will be shown in the area for the "Changed but not updated" part on the output for the "git status" command:

```
$ rm PROJECTS.md
$ git status
On branch master
Your branch is up-to-date with 'origin/master'.
Changes not staged for commit:
  (use "git add/rm <file>..." to update what will be committed)
  (use "git checkout -- <file>..." to discard changes in working directory)

    deleted:   PROJECTS.md
no changes added to commit (use "git add" and/or "git commit -a")
```

If you execute the "git rm" command, the removal will be staged as shown below:

```
$ git rm PROJECTS.md
rm 'PROJECTS.md'
$ git status
On branch master
Your branch is up-to-date with 'origin/master'.
Changes to be committed:
  (use "git reset HEAD <file>..." to unstage)

    deleted:   PROJECTS.md
```

Moving Files

Git will not track the movement of files. The "mv" command in Git is used for the purpose of renaming files. The command takes the syntax given below:

```
$ git mv file_from file_to
```

After running a command similar to the one given above, and then executing the command for status, you will see that the command is under renamed:

$ git mv README.md README
$ git status
On branch master
Your branch is up-to-date with 'origin/master'.
Changes to be committed:
  (use "git reset HEAD <file>..." to unstage)

  renamed: README.md -> README

The example given below best demonstrates this:

$ mv README.md README
$ git rm README.md
$ git add README

Chapter 2- Distributed and Centralized Workflow

Git provides you with distributed workflows. In a distributed Git workflow, one can participate either as a contributor or as an integrator. With this type of structure, one finds himself being very flexible in terms of whether he participates in a project.

In the case of a centralized workflow, each user is taken as an independent node working on a central hub. The problem is that in Git, one is potentially acting as a hub as well as a node. This is because one is allowed to make a contribution on a central repository or maintain a public repository which others will be able to access and make a contribution to.

Contributing to a project

There are a number of variations on how contribution to a project is done. Git offers much flexibility, and this is why the members of a development team can choose to do it in the way that they want. Some variables involved include active contributor count, chosen workflow, your commit access, and the external contribution method.

The active contributor count specifies the number of members who are actively contributing code to a project. In most cases, you will have one to two contributors, and these will be making a few commits in a day.

The workflow in the use of the project specifies whether the project is centralized with each member having equal rights to access to the main codeline, or whether there is an integration manager or maintainer who regularly checks for all the patches.

Commit access is also another issue. It will specify how you have contributed to the project if you have no write access to the project. Is there a policy for the project? It also specifies the amount of work that you contribute at a time, and what you do so as to contribute.

Private Small Team

In most cases, you will encounter a small project in which one or two contributors are participating. Suppose that we have two developers who are working on a shared repository. Let us see how they do it. The first user, Nicoh, begins by cloning the repository, makes some change, and then commits it locally. This is shown below:

```
# Nicoh's Machine
$ git clone nicoh@githost:simplegit.git
```

Cloning into 'simplegit'...

...

```
$ cd simplegit/
$ vim lib/simplegit.rb
$ git commit -am 'removed invalid default value'
[master 738ee87] removed invalid default value
 1 files changed, 1 insertions(+), 1 deletions(-)
```

The second user, Mercy, will do the same thing, clone the repository, and then commit the change. This is shown below:

```
# Mercy's Machine
$ git clone mercy@githost:simplegit.git
Cloning into 'simplegit'...
...
$ cd simplegit/
$ vim TODO
$ git commit -am 'add reset task'
[master fbff5bc] add reset task
 1 files changed, 1 insertions(+), 0 deletions(-)
```

Mercy will then push the work she has done to the server. This is shown below:

```
# Mercy's Machine
$ git push origin master
...
To mercy@githost:simplegit.git
   1edee6b..fbff5bc  master -> master
```

Nicoh then tries to push his work too. This is shown below:

```
# Nicoh's Machine
$ git push origin master
To nicoh@githost:simplegit.git
 ! [rejected]      master -> master (non-fast forward)
error: failed to push some refs to
'nicoh@githost:simplegit.git'
```

Nicoh is not allowed to push the work because Mercy has already done it. This is good for you to understand how Subversion works. This is because the two developers, Nicoh and Mercy, did not edit a similar file. In most cases, the Subversion will merge the two files which are edited on the server side. However, in the case of Git, the changes have to be committed manually. For Nicoh to push the changes to the server, he has to pull the changes from Mercy and then merge in as shown below:

$ git fetch origin
...
From nicoh@githost:simplegit
 + 049d078...fbff5bc master   -> origin/master

Nicoh has a reference to the changes made by Mercy, but he is supposed to merge them into his own work before pushing them. This is shown below:

$ git merge origin/master
Merge made by recursive.
 TODO | 1 +
 1 files changed, 1 insertions(+), 0 deletions(-)

The merge should run successfully. At this point, Nicoh can test his code so as to be sure that it works as expected, and the new work can then be pushed up to the server:

$ git push origin master
...
To nicoh@githost:simplegit.git
  fbff5bc..72bbc59 master -> master

During that period, Mercy was working on a topic branch. She has made another branch named "issue3" and three commits have been done on that branch. The changes made by Nicoh are yet to be fetched. For Mercy to sync with Nicoh, she has to fetch as follows:

```
# Mercy's Machine
$ git fetch origin
...
From mercy@githost:simplegit
  fbff5bc..72bbc59  master    -> origin/master
```

Mercy needs to know what she is supposed to merge so that she can push up. She executes the "git log" command as follows:

```
$ git log --no-merges issue54..origin/master
commit
738ee872852dfaa9d6634e0dea7a324040193016

Author: Nicholas Samuel <nicoh@example.com>
Date:   Fri May 17 16:02:56 2016 -0700

  removed invalid default value
```

She then switches to her master branch. Merge Nicoh's work into her master branch, and then push it back to her server. This is shown below:

```
$ git checkout master
Switched to branch 'master'
Your branch is behind 'origin/master' by 2 commits,
and can be fast-forwarded.
```

The merging can now be done with "issue3" or "origin/master" first. If she needs to merge with the "issue3" first, it should be as follows:

```
$ git merge issue54
Updating fbff5bc..4af4298
Fast forward
 README        |  1 +
 lib/simplegit.rb |  6 +++++-
 2 files changed, 6 insertions(+), 1 deletions(-)
```

At this point, Mercy can merge with Nicoh's work as shown below:

$ git merge origin/master
Auto-merging lib/simplegit.rb
Merge made by recursive.
 lib/simplegit.rb | 2 +-
 1 files changed, 1 insertions(+), 1 deletions(-)

And then Mercy is in a position to push, which can be done as shown below:

$ git push origin master
...
To mercy@githost:simplegit.git
  72bbc59..8059c15 master -> master

Chapter 3- Conflicts

Most conflicts which occur in Git can be resolved via the command line. However, in the case of certain conflicts, you will be expected to have a text editor.

Creation of an Edit Collision

This is the type of conflict which occurs most frequently. It occurs when two parts of a file are changed by two branches, and then the branches are joined together. To know more about the conflict, you have to run the "git status" command. This is shown below:

$ git status
 # On branch branch-b
 # You have unmerged paths.
 #   (fix conflicts and run "git commit")
#
 # Unmerged paths:
 #   (use "git add ..." to mark resolution)
#
 # both modified: planets.md
#
no changes added to commit (use "git add" and/or "git commit -a")

Suppose two users have modified the file "PLANETS.MD." ONCE YOU OPEN THE FILE ON A TEXT EDITOR, YOU GET THE FOLLOWING:

the number of planets are
<<<<<<< HEAD
nine
=======
seven
>>>>>>> branch-a

For the "branch –a" part, you wrote nine, but the other user wrote seven. Git will automatically add the conflict markers to the areas which are affected. An area which is conflict marked begins with "<<<<<<<" and then ends with ">>>>>>>." These are referred to as the conflict markers. The two conflicting blocks have to be divided by use of "=======."

You can choose to keep the changes, take the changes from your friend, or just make a new change. However, it is good for you to take a step which will leave the file okay and everyone happy. You will have to put a new version for the line which was affected. You goal should be to have the file look exactly the way that you want. The conflict markers should be deleted, and then a new change written. This is shown below:

the number of planets are
nine, or eight, depending on who you ask.

After that, the command "git add" can be done for the file, the changes committed with a new commit message, and all will be okay.

Resolving Removed File Conflict

This type of conflict occurs when an individual edits a particular file, and then that individual deletes the file from their branch. Git will not know whether you need to keep that particular file with the edits, or just to delete the file and then keep the edits.

How to Keep the Edited File

First, you can resolve the conflict just by maintaining the changes. Suppose a new file had been added to the file README.MD in "branch-b," but someone else has deleted the file in "branch-c." Git will declare the conflict given below:

CONFLICT (modify/delete): README.md deleted in HEAD and modified in branch-b. Version branch-b of README.md left in tree.

Automatic merge failed; fix conflicts and then commit the result.

```
git status
# On branch branch-c
# You have unmerged paths.
#   (fix conflicts and run "git commit")
#
# Unmerged paths:
#     (use "git add/rm ..." as appropriate to mark
resolution)
#
# deleted by us:    README.md
#
no changes added to commit (use "git add" and/or
"git commit -a")
```

The conflict can be resolved by adding the file back and then committing the changes:

$ git add README.md

$ git commit
[branch-c 9bc3b01] Merge branch 'branch-b' into branch-c

```
git show | head
commit
9bc3b013ofe0178359d51243b5b882076a12f554
Merge: 4c80a63 7e8b679
Author: Nicoh :sam:
Date:   Sat Jun 1 18:39:40 2013 -0700
```

**   Merge branch 'branch-b' into branch-c**
>
**   Conflicts:**
**   README.md**

Removing the File to Resolve the Conflict

In this case, you resolve the conflict by leaving the file deleted. When a merge conflict occurs, Git will declare the following:

CONFLICT (modify/delete): README.md deleted in HEAD and modified in branch-c. Version branch-c of README.md left in tree.

Automatic merge failed; fix conflicts and then commit the result.

git status
 # On branch branch-d
 # You have unmerged paths.
 #   (fix conflicts and run "git commit")
#
 # Unmerged paths:
 #   (use "git add/rm ..." as appropriate to mark resolution)
#
 #   deleted by us: README.md
#
no changes added to commit (use "git add" and/or "git commit -a")

Now, you need to remove the file using the "Git rm" command. This can be done as follows:

git rm README.md
README.md: needs merge
rm 'README.md'

It will then be good, and you can commit using the default message. This is shown below:

git commit
[branch-d 6f89e49] Merge branch 'branch-c' into branch-d

git show | head
commit
6f89e49189ba3a2b7440fc434f351cb041b3999e
Merge: 211261b fcc1093
Author: nicoh :sam:
Date: Sat Jun 1 18:43:01 2013 -0700

    Merge branch 'branch-c' into branch-d
>
    Conflicts:
      README.md

Chapter 4- Submodules and Hooks

Whenever you are working on a particular project, you will always need to access another project from that one. In Git, this issue is addressed by the use of submodules. These allow one to keep a Git repository as another Git repository or as a subdirectory. With that, you will clone your other repository into the project and then keep your commits separate.

Starting with Submodules

We want to create a project having a major project and some sub-projects. We should begin by adding an existing Git repository such as a submodule of the respository we are working on. If you need to add a submodule, you have to use the "git submodule ads" command while specifying the absolute or relative path of the project which we need to begin tracking. In our case, we need to add a library named "DbConnector." This is shown below:

$ git submodule add
https://github.com/chaconinc/DbConnector
Cloning into 'DbConnector'...
remote: Counting objects: 11, done.
remote: Compressing objects: 100% (10/10), done.
remote: Total 11 (delta 0), reused 11 (delta 0)
Unpacking objects: 100% (11/11), done.
Checking connectivity... done.

A different path can be added to the end of the file if you need to go into another directory. Once you execute the "git status" command at this point, you will see the following information:

$ git status
On branch master
Your branch is up-to-date with 'origin/master'.

Changes to be committed:
  (use "git reset HEAD <file>..." to unstage)

new file: .gitmodules
new file: DbConnector

You should have noticed that you have a new file that is ".gitmodules." This is just a configuration project which specifies the mapping which takes place between the local subdirectory which you have pulled into and the URL for the project. This is shown below:

[submodule "DbConnector"]
path = DbConnector
url = https://github.com/chaconinc/DbConnector

The output for the "git status" command also shows the project folder entry. Running the command "git diff" on that will give you the following:

$ git diff --cached DbConnector
diff --git a/DbConnector b/DbConnector
new file mode 160000
index 0000000..c3f01dc
--- /dev/null
+++ b/DbConnector
@@ -0,0 +1 @@
+Subproject commit
c3f01dc8862123d317dd46284b05b6892c7b29bc

Although the "Dbconnector" is a subdirectory in our working directory, Git will see it as a submodule, and it will not track its contents when you are not in the directory. If you want to get a nicer output from the command, add the --submodule flag to the command. This is shown below:

$ git diff --cached --submodule
diff --git a/.gitmodules b/.gitmodules
new file mode 100644
index 0000000..71fc376
--- /dev/null
+++ b/.gitmodules

```
@@ -0,0 +1,3 @@
+[submodule "DbConnector"]
+    path = DbConnector
+    url =
https://github.com/chaconinc/DbConnector
Submodule DbConnector 0000000...c3f01dc (new
submodule)
```

After a commit, you will see something like what is given below:

```
$ git commit -am 'added DbConnector module'
[master fb9093c] added DbConnector module
 2 files changed, 4 insertions(+)
 create mode 100644 .gitmodules
 create mode 160000 DbConnector
```

How to Clone a Project with Submodules

We want to clone a project which has a submodule in it. Once you clone such a project, you get directories with the submodules, but no files in them. This is shown below:

```
$ git clone
https://github.com/chaconinc/MainProject

Cloning into 'MainProject'...
remote: Counting objects: 14, done.
remote: Compressing objects: 100% (13/13), done.
remote: Total 14 (delta 1), reused 13 (delta 0)
Unpacking objects: 100% (14/14), done.
Checking connectivity... done.
$ cd MainProject
$ ls -la
total 16
drwxr-xr-x   9 schacon  staff  306 Sep 17 15:21 .
drwxr-xr-x   7 schacon  staff  238 Sep 17 15:21 ..
drwxr-xr-x  13 schacon  staff  442 Sep 17 15:21 .git
-rw-r--r--   1 schacon  staff   92 Sep 17 15:21
.gitmodules

drwxr-xr-x   2 schacon  staff   68 Sep 17 15:21
DbConnector

-rw-r--r--   1 schacon  staff  756 Sep 17 15:21 Makefile
drwxr-xr-x   3 schacon  staff  102 Sep 17 15:21 includes
drwxr-xr-x   4 schacon  staff  136 Sep 17 15:21 scripts
drwxr-xr-x   4 schacon  staff  136 Sep 17 15:21 src
$ cd DbConnector/
$ ls
$
```

We have the Dbconnector directory, but it is now empty. Two commands have to be executed, that is, "git submodule init" for initializing the configuration file, and the command "git submodule update" for fetching all of your data from the project and then check for the commit listed in the superproject. This is shown below:

$ git submodule init
Submodule 'DbConnector'
(https://github.com/chaconinc/DbConnector)
registered for path 'DbConnector'

$ git submodule update
Cloning into 'DbConnector'...
remote: Counting objects: 11, done.
remote: Compressing objects: 100% (10/10), done.
remote: Total 11 (delta 0), reused 11 (delta 0)
Unpacking objects: 100% (11/11), done.
Checking connectivity... done.
Submodule path 'DbConnector': checked out
'c3f01dc8862123d317dd46284b05b6892c7b29bc'

In case you pass the flag "—recursive" to the "git clone" command, each submodule contained in the repository will automatically be initialized and updated. This is shown below:

$ git clone --recursive
https://github.com/chaconinc/MainProject
Cloning into 'MainProject'...
remote: Counting objects: 14, done.
remote: Compressing objects: 100% (13/13), done.
remote: Total 14 (delta 1), reused 13 (delta 0)
Unpacking objects: 100% (14/14), done.
Checking connectivity... done.
Submodule 'DbConnector'
(https://github.com/chaconinc/DbConnector)
registered for path 'DbConnector'

Cloning into 'DbConnector'...

remote: Counting objects: 11, done.
remote: Compressing objects: 100% (10/10), done.
remote: Total 11 (delta 0), reused 11 (delta 0)
Unpacking objects: 100% (11/11), done.
Checking connectivity... done.
Submodule path 'DbConnector': checked out
'c3f01dc8862123d317dd46284b05b6892c7b29bc'

Git Hooks

Hooks are used for firing off custom scripts when some important actions do occur. Hooks are of two types, client-side and server-side. The client-side hooks are triggered by operations such as merging and committing, while server-side hooks are triggered by operations such as receiving of pushed commits.

The hooks are usually stored in the "hooks" subdirectory of the Git repository. In most of the projects, this is the ".git/hooks."

Committing-Workflow Hooks

We use four hooks when committing on the client side. Let us discuss these:

1. pre-commit- this hook is run first before we can even write in the commit message. We use it for inspecting the snapshot which is just to be committed, so as to be sure that nothing has been left, and that the tests can run well. You also have to examine whatever you have in your code.

2. prepare-commit-msg- this has to be executed before firing up of the commit message editor and after creation of the default message. It will allow you to edit the default message before the commit author can see it. This type of hook usually takes in some parameters which include the path to the file which is holding the commit message, the commit type, and the SHA-1 if the commit is an amended one. This type of hook is not very useful when it comes to the normal commits, but it is good when it comes to hooks where the commit message is auto-generated such as in merge commits, template commit messages, amended commits, and squashed commits.

3. commit-msg- this type of hook takes only a single parameter, which is the path to our temporary file which has the commit message which has been written by the developer. In case the script exits nonzero, Git will abort the commit process, meaning that you will be in a position to validate the project state, or the commit message before the commit can be allowed to go through.

The "post-commit" will be run once the commit process has completed. This type of commit will take no arguments, but if you need to get the last commit, you just have to run the command "git log -1 HEAD." The script is generally used for notification purposes, or for something which is similar to that.

The following are the server-side hooks:

1. pre-receive- this is the first script to run when one is handling a push from the client side. It usually takes in a list of references pushed from the stdin. This hook can be used for purposes such as performing access control for all refs and files which are being modified via the push.

2. Update- this one is similar is similar to the above hook, with the exception being that it is run only once for each of the branches that the pusher is trying to update. In case the pusher tries to update many branches, the hook will run only once, while the update will run only once per branch that they are pushing to.

3. post-receive- this script will run once the entire script has been completed and this can be used for the purpose of notifying other users or for updating the other services. The hook will take the same stdin data as the post-receive hook.

Chapter 5- Conversion of a Subversion Repository into Git

We need to demonstrate how conversion works from a subversion repository to a Git repository which is sharable with others. Bare repositories usually work without any local checkouts for the files which are available for modifications. They form the format which is highly recommended for the shared repositories.

1. Begin by retrieving the list of all the Subversion committers
   The Subversion lists the username for each of the commits. The commits for Git are usually rich in data, but the author will need to have both the username and the email listed. The default setting is that the tool "git-svn" lists the username in both your username and email fields. However, when you work on it a bit, it will be possible for you to add all the SVN users as well as their corresponding usernames and emails. The git-svn can then make use of that list so as to transform the plain svn usernames into the proper Git committers.

   Run the command given below from the root of the local Subversion checkout:

   svn log -q | awk -F '|' '/^r/ {sub("^ ", "", $2); sub(" $", "", $2); print $2" = "$2" <"$2">"}' | sort -u > authors-transform.txt

   The above command will grab all the log messages, pluck out usernames, remove any duplicate usernames, sort usernames, and lastly place them in the file "authors-transform.txt." You can then edit each of the lines contained in the file.

2. Use git-svn to clone the Subversion repository
   The command can be used as shown below:

git svn clone [SVN repo URL] --no-metadata -A authors-transform.txt --stdlayout ~/temp

The above command will perform a very standard git-svn transformation and then place the Git repository in the "~/temp" folder in our home directory. This will be done using the text file we had created earlier on.

3. Convert the svn:ignore properties to .gitignore
   If your repository was using the properties for "svn:ignore," this can easily be converted into a ".gitignore" as shown below:

cd ~/temp
git svn show-ignore > .gitignore
git add .gitignore
git commit -m 'Convert svn:ignore properties to .gitignore.'

4. Push the repository to a bare Git repository
   Begin by creating a bare repository, and then make a default match for it. This is shown below:

git init --bare ~/new-bare.git
cd ~/new-bare.git
git symbolic-ref HEAD refs/heads/trunk

The temp repository can then be pushed to the bare repository as shown below:

cd ~/temp
git remote add bare ~/new-bare.git
git config remote.bare.push 'refs/remotes/*:refs/heads/*'
git push bare

The ~/temp repository can now be safely deleted.

5. Rename the "trunk" branch to "master" branch
   The main development branch in your project will be the trunk which will match the name which you had in the Subversion. This will have to be renamed into the Git master branch as shown below:

   cd ~/new-bare.git
   git branch -m trunk master

6. Clean the branches and tags
   The git-svn will make all of your Subversion tags to be short branches in the Git of "tags/name" form. These branches will have to be converted into the actual Git tags by use of the following command:

   cd ~/new-bare.git
   git for-each-ref --format='%(refname)'
   refs/heads/tags |
   cut -d / -f 4 |
   while read ref
   do
     git tag "$ref" "refs/heads/tags/$ref";
     git branch -D "tags/$ref";
   done

   You will have to do some bit of typing in this step, but do not be worried. After completing it, you will be done.

Chapter 6- Contributing to a Project

Follow the steps given below:

1. Set up a functional copy on your computer
A local fork for the project is needed first. Open Github and then click on the "fork" button. A copy of the repository will then be created in your own Github account, and a forked note will be seen underneath the project.

   A copy is needed locally, so look for "SSH clone URL" in your right hand column, and then use it for cloning locally in the terminal:

$ git clone git@github.com:akrabat/zend-validator.git

   Change the directory to your new project:

$ cd zend-validator
Create a new remote and give it the name "upstream":

$ git remote add upstream git@github.com:zendframework/zend-validator.git

2. Perform a task
Assuming that we need to fix a bug found in the zend-validator, we begin by branching from the master as follows:

$ git checkout master
$ git pull upstream master && git push origin master
$ git checkout -b hotfix/readme-update

3. Create the PR

For you to create the PR, you have to push the branch to the origin remote, and then click on some buttons on the Github. The following command can be used for pushing the new branch:

$ git push -u origin hotfix/readme-update

The branch will then be created on your Github project. The use of the −u flag is to link this branch to the remote one,

4. Review by the maintainers

   For your work to be made part of the project, the maintainers will have to review it and decide whether to request some changes or merge it.

You will then be done.

Conclusion

We have come to the end of this guide. My hope is that you are now aware of how to use Git. For you to be able to use Git, you should begin by installing it on your local computer. Installation instructions exist on how to install this on the various platforms such as Windows, Linux, and Mac OS X. These have been discussed in this book. The workflow in Git is organized in a distributed or centralized manner. This determines how the users or those participating in a project make their contribution. Normally, the Git project can either be private or public. When you are working on a particular project in Git, you may need to access another project in Git. This is usually done by the use of Submodules. This book has explored how to do this, and by now, you should be aware of how to do it. Projects in Git are sharable, and this is why we should convert subversion repositories into Git. Of course, when using Git, you will need to contribute to the ongoing projects. There are steps which should be followed for this to be done, and these have been explained here.

www.ingramcontent.com/pod-product-compliance
Lightning Source LLC
Chambersburg PA
CBHW070902070326
40690CB00009B/1959